This Sticker Book belongs to:

_____

_____

_____

My Lovely Stickers

My Lovely Stickers

My Lovely Stickers

My Lovely Stickers

My Lovely Stickers

My Lovely Stickers

My Lovely Stickers

My Lovely Stickers

My Lovely Stickers

My Lovely Stickers

My Lovely Stickers

My Lovely Stickers

My Lovely Stickers

My Lovely Stickers

My Lovely Stickers

My Lovely Stickers

My Lovely Stickers

My Lovely Stickers

My Lovely Stickers

My Lovely Stickers

My Lovely Stickers

My Lovely Stickers

My Lovely Stickers

My Lovely Stickers

My Lovely Stickers

My Lovely Stickers

My Lovely Stickers

My Lovely Stickers

My Lovely Stickers

My Lovely Stickers

My Lovely Stickers

My Lovely Stickers

My Lovely Stickers

My Lovely Stickers

My Lovely Stickers

My Lovely Stickers

My Lovely Stickers

My Lovely Stickers

My Lovely Stickers

My Lovely Stickers

My Lovely Stickers

My Lovely Stickers

My Lovely Stickers

My Lovely Stickers

My Lovely Stickers

My Lovely Stickers

My Lovely Stickers

My Lovely Stickers

My Lovely Stickers

My Lovely Stickers

My Lovely Stickers

My Lovely Stickers

My Lovely Stickers

My Lovely Stickers

My Lovely Stickers

My Lovely Stickers

My Lovely Stickers

My Lovely Stickers

My Lovely Stickers

My Lovely Stickers

My Lovely Stickers

My Lovely Stickers

My Lovely Stickers

My Lovely Stickers

My Lovely Stickers

My Lovely Stickers

My Lovely Stickers

My Lovely Stickers

My Lovely Stickers

My Lovely Stickers

My Lovely Stickers

My Lovely Stickers

My Lovely Stickers

My Lovely Stickers

My Lovely Stickers

My Lovely Stickers

My Lovely Stickers

My Lovely Stickers

My Lovely Stickers

My Lovely Stickers

My Lovely Stickers

My Lovely Stickers

My Lovely Stickers

My Lovely Stickers

My Lovely Stickers

My Lovely Stickers

My Lovely Stickers

My Lovely Stickers

My Lovely Stickers

My Lovely Stickers

My Lovely Stickers

My Lovely Stickers

My Lovely Stickers

My Lovely Stickers

My Lovely Stickers

My Lovely Stickers

My Lovely Stickers

My Lovely Stickers

Made in the USA
Monee, IL
21 November 2020